# A NOTE TO PARENTS ABOUT FIGHTING

Differences often lead to disagreements. Disagreements often lead to arguments. Arguments often lead to fights. While disagreements, and even arguments, are an inevitable part of human relationships, fighting is not. Fights occur only when people are unwilling or unable to resolve their differences peacefully. The purpose of this book is to explain how fights originate, how they can be avoided, and how they can be handled if and when they occur. Reading and discussing this book with your child can spare him or her from the negative consequences of fighting.

It is important to teach your child that it is okay for people to be different from one another. It is also okay for people to disagree. However, it is not okay for people to engage in arguments or fights in which anyone is hurt or property is damaged or destroyed.

Realizing that there are always two sides to every argument, and encouraging your child to try to understand both sides, is crucial to helping him or her resolve differences before they turn into fights. Understanding the other person's point of view is something you need to demonstrate. Only then will your child embrace this important social concept and integrate it into the way he or she relates to others.

This book belongs to:

Melissa

Published by Scholastic Inc.
90 Old Sherman Turnpike, Danbury, CT  06816.

SCHOLASTIC and associated logos are trademarks and/or
registered trademarks of Scholastic Inc.

ISBN 0-7172-8584-7

First Scholastic Printing, October 2005

# A Book About
# Fighting

by
**Joy Berry**

**SCHOLASTIC INC.**

New York   Toronto   London   Auckland   Sydney
Mexico City   New Delhi   Hong Kong   Buenos Aires

This book is about T. J. and his sister, Tami.

Reading about T. J. and Tami can help you understand and deal with **fighting.**

Sometimes people get angry and want to fight. When people fight:

- They can hurt each other's bodies.
- They can hurt each other's feelings.
- They can damage or destroy each other's belongings and things around them.

*Never do anything to hurt yourself or another person.* Do not hit, kick, bite, pinch, or pull anyone's hair.

*Never damage or destroy things.* Do not hit, kick, or throw things that can be broken or ruined.

Try to avoid fighting. Stay away from people who always make you angry.

Try to avoid fighting. Do not play too roughly. Someone usually gets hurt when people play roughly. The person who is hurt may get angry and want to fight.

Try to avoid fighting. Do not spend too much time with one person. People often fight when they get tired of being around each other.

Ask your parent or someone else to help you if you and the other person cannot decide what to do.

Listen to the person's advice, and then follow it.

You can solve the problems you have with other people without fighting.

If someone does something that makes you angry, do not do anything right away. You might get into a fight if you act too quickly.

Slowly count to ten when you are angry to give yourself time to calm down.

When you are calm, talk with the person who made you angry. Do not scream. Do not say mean things.

Talk about how you feel. Explain why you are angry. Tell the person what you think should be done.

Give the other person a chance to talk.
Listen carefully. Show respect for the other
person's thoughts and feelings. Try to
understand the other person's point of
view.

Decide what to do about the problem after you and the other person have said what needs to be said. There are at least three ways to solve a problem:

- You can do what the other person wants to do.
- The other person can do what you want to do.
- You both can give in some without giving in completely. This is called *compromising*.

Ask your parent or someone else to help you if you and the other person cannot decide what to do.

Listen to the person's advice, and then follow it.

Fighting can be harmful. When you fight, you might hurt yourself or others. You might damage or destroy something.

That is why you should not fight.

It is best for everyone when problems are solved without fighting.